KNOW THE FACTS

DRUGS

Sarah Medina

WAYLAND

Wayland
338 Euston Road
London NW1 3BH

Wayland Australia
Level 17/207 Kent Street
Sydney, NSW 2000

Series editor: Nicola Edwards
Consultant: David Ferguson
Designer: Jason Anscomb
Picture researcher: Kathy Lockley

All pictures posed by models. The author and publisher would like to thank the models and the
following for allowing their pictures to be reproduced in this publication: Pepo Alcala/Alamy: 16;
Keven Dodge/Corbis: 44; A. Glauberman/Science Photo Library: 19; David Hoffman/Photofusion: 14;
Jennifer Jaquemart/Rex Features: 35; Kutting-People/Alamy: 18; By Ian Miles – Flashpoint
Pictures/Alamy: 13; Pablo Paul/Alamy: 12; PYMCA/Alamy: 4; Rex Features: 43; Karen
Robinson/Photofusion: 41; Sakki/Rex Features: 31; Tom Stewart/Corbis: 27; Paul
Underhill/PYMCA/Jupiterimages: 8; Wayland Archive: 11; Janine Wiedel Photolibrary/Alamy: 25;
Wishlist: 5, 7, 9, 10, 17, 20, 21, 22, 23, 26, 28, 32, 34, 36, 37, 39, 40; WoodyStock/Alamy: 45

British Library Cataloguing in Publication Data
 Medina, Sarah
    Drugs. - (Know the facts)
    1. Drug abuse - Juvenile literature
    I. Title
    362.2'9
ISBN: 978 0 7502 5387 1
Printed in China

Wayland is a division of Hachette Children's Books,
an Hachette Livre UK company.
www.hachettelivre.co.uk

CONTENTS

Drugs in everyday life 4

What are drugs? 6

Why do people use drugs? 8

Are drugs safe? 10

Stimulants 12
Cocaine
Crack cocaine
Ecstasy
Anabolic steroids
Tobacco

Depressants 20
Alcohol
Cannabis
Volatile substances

Hallucinogens and analgesics 30
LSD
Heroin

Problem drug use 32

Worried about someone? 35

Getting help 37

In an emergency 41

Making the right choices 43

Glossary 46

Further information 47

Index 48

DRUGS IN EVERYDAY LIFE

Drugs are all around us. Anyone who has drunk coffee, tea, chocolate or cola has taken a drug called caffeine. Many millions of people use the drug tobacco whenever they light up a cigarette, or use the drug alcohol when they enjoy wine or beer. Even people who are ill and who take medicines given by their doctor, or which they buy at a chemist's, could be called drug users! All these drugs are legal, but they still affect people's bodies and minds.

People use illegal drugs, such as cannabis, cocaine and heroin, too. Young people are often tempted to use drugs by their friends. They may think that drugs will help them to have more fun or to escape from their problems.

Drugs such as alcohol and tobacco are a common part of the 'party scene'. People may take drugs to help them feel relaxed and confident in social situations or to 'fit in' with a group of their peers.

- The most common drugs in use today include cannabis, tobacco, alcohol, Ecstasy and cocaine.

Illegal drugs

All drugs can be harmful, but illegal drugs can be especially damaging to people's health. Legal drugs are controlled to make them safer. Illegal drugs may be very strong or impure, making them dangerous to use. The illegal drugs world is not a safe place, and buying drugs can be risky. Some drug users turn to crime themselves, so

they can buy the drugs they become addicted to. It is for all these reasons that these types of drugs are made illegal.

Nothing new

There is nothing new about drug use. Since the earliest times, people all around the world have turned to drugs to relax, forget their worries or cure their illnesses. At first, drugs came from plants. We know that, 7000 years ago, the Sumerian people used a drug called opium, which comes from poppies; they called it 'joy'.

Today, people use legal and illegal drugs every day. Most do so safely and without getting into trouble. Others suffer serious physical, psychological or emotional harm. Sadly, some die.

Find out more

In this book, readers will find down-to-earth, accurate information about drugs. The book explores why people use drugs, and the effects and risks of doing so. Readers will also find out where they can find help for drug problems.

Some drugs are easily available – and cheap enough for young people to afford. Sometimes young people may be offered drugs outside the gates of their school.

HAVE YOUR SAY

"My dad smokes a pack of cigarettes a day. He says he can't give up smoking."

"My sister says she can't start the day until she's had a cup of coffee."

WHAT ARE DRUGS?

A drug is a natural or chemical substance that changes how someone feels. Legal drugs include caffeine, tobacco, alcohol and medicines. Chemicals that are found in schools and homes, such as gases, glues and aerosols, are legal, but can be misused as drugs. Illegal drugs include cannabis, cocaine, Ecstasy, LSD and heroin.

It is easy to come across most legal drugs. Children can buy glues and aerosols, and some medicines, from shops and supermarkets. In the UK, anyone over the age of 18 can buy alcohol and cigarettes. People purchase illegal drugs from drug dealers. Some people share their drugs with friends.

WHAT'S THE PROBLEM?

'My friends at school are talking about trying drugs. They say lots of people take drugs for fun and don't come to any harm. I don't know what to say to them.'

People who use drugs 'for fun' often choose their drug depending on how they want to feel. They may think that cannabis will relax them or that Ecstasy will give them a buzz. But this is not always easy to predict. The effect of a drug can vary, depending on someone's mood, who they are with and where they are when they use the drug. Problem drug users may mix different types of drugs. This can be very dangerous indeed.

As you read this book, you'll find out a lot of information about the effects of different drugs and the consequences of taking them.

Most drugs fall into one of four categories, depending on the effects they have when people take them.

Stimulants

Stimulants, or 'uppers', speed up people's bodies, making them feel excited and energetic. Caffeine, tobacco, cocaine, Ecstasy and anabolic steroids are all stimulants. (See pages 12-19 for more information.)

Depressants

As the name suggests, depressants, or 'downers', have the opposite effect on the body as stimulants. They slow people down, and make them feel drowsy and relaxed. Depressants include alcohol, cannabis and volatile substances. (See pages 20-29 for more information.)

Hallucinogens

Hallucinogens, or 'trips', make people hallucinate, which means that they see or hear things that are not really there. LSD and magic mushrooms are both hallucinogens. (See page 30 for more information.)

Analgesics

Analgesics have a pain-killing effect. They may give people a 'warm glow', making them feel more relaxed. Analgesics include heroin and methadone. (See page 31 for more information.)

Young people sometimes misuse common products, such as glue. But sniffing glue can have dire consequences, and can kill someone on the spot.

It's a Fact ✓

- In the UK, drugs are Class A, Class B or Class C, depending on how harmful they are. Anyone who is caught with even a small amount of drugs will face consequences from the police – from a warning to imprisonment or a fine. The consequences for drug dealers are severe, and can include life in prison.

WHY DO PEOPLE USE DRUGS?

People of all ages use drugs – for all sorts of reasons. We all have natural brain chemicals that affect what we do, think and feel. Different drugs alter these chemicals in different ways. Stimulants, such as Ecstasy, can give people a real 'buzz'. Depressants, such as cannabis, can make people feel super-relaxed. Hallucinogens, such as LSD, give people exciting 'trips'. Analgesics, such as heroin, can slow people down and make them feel 'apart' from the real world. These effects can be very tempting.

Ecstasy can give clubbers a sense of euphoria and the energy to last the night.

Drugs for fun

Some young people are curious about what it feels like to take drugs. They experiment with one or several drugs to feel the 'thrills' drugs can give.

Drugs are sometimes linked to fashion, music and dance. Many people use drugs to relax, get 'high' or lose their inhibitions when they are socializing. For them, taking drugs equals fun.

HAVE YOUR SAY

"I first started doing Es when I was about 14. Everyone was doing it. All I remember is the first time I did it; it was amazing!"

Under pressure

'Come on! It's great!'. Many young people know what it is like to be pressurized by their friends to do or try something new. Some of them use drugs because their friends are doing it. They want to belong – to feel part of the group. They may want to rebel against their family or society. Taking drugs may make them feel cool and attractive.

A range of reasons

Some young people use drugs to escape from problems and bad experiences, such as abuse or neglect, at home or school. Others have low self-esteem, and want to feel better or to 'fit' better in society.

Young people see drug-taking as a common and acceptable thing to do. After all, they frequently see adults using alcohol or tobacco to wind down and relax. Like most adults, most young people do not use illegal drugs. If they do, it may only be for a short while. However, all drug use brings risks, and some young people get hooked and suffer serious consequences.

Some people use drugs, such as tobacco, that stop them from feeling hungry, so they do not gain weight.

What Would you do?

You look older than your friends, and they ask you to go into a supermarket to buy some cider. Do you:

(a) Get angry, shout 'No way!' and walk away.
(b) Feel scared, but go in and buy some, anyway.
(c) Say 'No' calmly, and explain that you don't want to get involved with underage drinking.

Turn to page 47 for the answers.

ARE DRUGS SAFE?

Some people drink wine with dinner every night, and find it relaxing and enjoyable. Others become alcoholics, ruining their lives. Some people smoke only with friends, ignoring cigarettes the rest of the time. Others become addicted and die of smoking-related illnesses. Although drugs can be used safely and in a controlled way, it is impossible to say that all drugs are 100% safe. Drugs bring risks. It is important to be aware of these risks in order to make good and sensible choices.

Smoking can cause potentially life-threatening lung diseases, such as asthma.

Health and sickness

Some drugs cause long-term health problems. Over time, alcohol can cause liver disease, and tobacco can cause lung cancer. Both can lead to a slow death. Death can come more quickly, too. Some people overdose on drugs, with no time to be rescued. The more someone uses a drug, the more of it they need to achieve the same effect. Addiction is a real risk.

Drug use can damage psychological health, too. Drugs can cause anxiety, paranoia or panic attacks, especially if there is a history of mental illness, such as depression, in the family.

It's a Fact

- Some young people have died from a heart attack after using drugs, especially volatile substances.

Money, money, money

A drug habit can be very expensive. Even though some drugs, such as Ecstasy and alcohol, are quite cheap, regular drug users often find themselves in debt. Some turn to crime to get the money they need to buy drugs.

Lost friends, lost lives

Drugs can ruin relationships. The bottom line with drugs is always the same: drugs before people. Someone who is addicted to drugs will not hesitate to hurt those they love – stealing from and lying to them – as long as they get their next 'fix'.

School and work can become difficult to cope with as drugs wear away people's memory and concentration. In addition, taking illegal drugs is breaking the law. People who get a police conviction can find it hard to get on in life.

Safe from danger?

People who are high on drugs are much more likely to get into trouble or to have an accident. They often take risky decisions, such as going home with someone they do not know, which put them in danger.

People who use drugs regularly can struggle to keep up with important schoolwork.

HAVE YOUR SAY

"I ran out of money, and that's when things got really bad. I stole from my mum and her friends when they visited our house and used the money to buy drugs."

STIMULANTS

People use stimulants, or 'uppers', to help them to feel excited and energetic. This part of the book examines some of the most common stimulants: cocaine, crack cocaine, Ecstasy, anabolic steroids and tobacco.

It's a Fact

COCAINE

Other names for cocaine
C, charlie, coke, snow, toot, white.

What is it?
Cocaine is made from the leaves of the coca plant.

What does it look like?
A white powder, often wrapped in small packets of paper or cling film.

How is it used?
Cocaine is sniffed up the nose. It can also be dissolved and injected.

What does it feel like?
Cocaine makes people feel full of energy and confidence. They get a sense of great well-being. These effects last for about 30 minutes.

What are the short-term risks?
Cocaine can make people feel nervous and panicky. Their heart rate and blood pressure may go up, and they may feel hot and restless. They may feel sick and find it hard to sleep.

What are the long-term risks?
People who use cocaine regularly may get chest pains and develop heart problems, which can kill them. Some people have convulsions. Others become paranoid. Injecting cocaine can damage people's veins. Cocaine is highly addictive.

The law
Cocaine is a Class A drug.

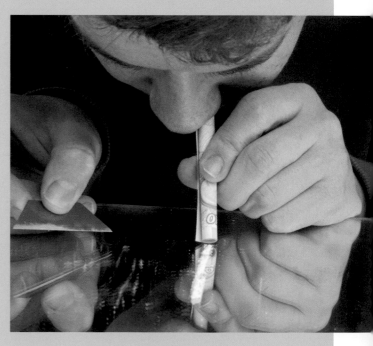

It's a Fact ✓

Other names for crack cocaine
Rock, stone, wash.

What is it?
Crack is a form of cocaine.

What does it look like?
Small crystals, which are the size of raisins.

How is it used?
Crack cocaine can be smoked. It can also be dissolved and injected into the body.

What does it feel like?
The effects of crack cocaine are similar to those of cocaine. The initial effects can be more powerful than cocaine, but they only last for a few minutes.

What are the short-term risks?
People who use crack cocaine may feel breathless and have chest pains. Their heart rate and blood pressure may go up, and they may feel hot and restless. They often feel sick. They can be tired, but not sleep properly. Some people become very paranoid and aggressive.

What are the long-term risks?
Smoking crack cocaine can cause breathing problems, including 'crack cough' and 'crack lung'. This is a highly addictive and expensive drug.

The law
Crack cocaine is a Class A drug.

WHAT'S THE PROBLEM? 😫

'Is it safe to inject drugs?'

Injecting drugs always brings extra risks. It can damage veins and cause ulcers. Sharing needles puts people at risk of catching serious infections, such as hepatitis and HIV/AIDS.

ECSTASY

Other names for Ecstasy

E, brownies, burgers, hug drug, pills.

What is it?

Ecstasy is a synthetic drug.

What does it look like?

Ecstasy comes in tablets of different shapes, sizes and colours, or as a powder.

How is it used?

It is swallowed.

What does it feel like?

People who take Ecstasy often feel full of energy. They lose all their inhibitions and feel friendly towards everybody. Sounds, colours and emotions all seem more intense. These effects last for 3-6 hours. After the high, people often feel very calm.

What are the short-term risks?

Some Ecstasy users feel frightened and panicky. Because they are 'spaced out', they are more likely to have an accident. Because they feel they can dance for hours, they may become dangerously dehydrated. People who use Ecstasy should sip no more than one pint of a non-alcoholic drink, such as water or fruit juice, every hour. Drinking too much liquid quickly can be as dangerous as not drinking at all.

People can die after taking Ecstasy for the first time. The comedown after using Ecstasy can last for several days.

What are the long-term risks?

Ecstasy can cause liver, kidney and heart problems. Users may suffer memory loss or develop mental illness, such as depression.

The law

Ecstasy is a Class A drug.

ANABOLIC STEROIDS

Other names for anabolic steroids

250, Anavar, Deca-Durabolin, Dianabol, 'Roids, Sustanon, Stanozolol.

What are they?

Anabolic steroids are chemicals that are related to the male sex hormone testosterone.

What do they look like?

Anabolic steroids come as tablets or as an oily-looking liquid.

How are they used?

Tablets are swallowed; liquids are injected into muscles.

What do they feel like?

Anabolic steroids make people feel as if they can train harder, which is why they are popular with athletes. They make muscles bigger and stronger, and help people to recover faster after doing lots of exercise. However, athletes who use anabolic steroids risk being banned from their sport.

What are the short-term risks?

Anabolic steroids can make people confused, paranoid and aggressive, even if they are usually calm. They may feel very tired after taking steroids, but find it hard to sleep.

What are the long-term risks?

Anabolic steroids can cause high blood pressure, and heart and liver problems. They can stop young people from growing properly; girls can grow more body hair and boys may develop breasts.

The law

Anabolic steroids are a Class C drug.

HAVE YOUR SAY

"I took a couple of Es on a night out and had a great time. But the comedown was the worst ever. I could hardly get out of bed for a couple of days, and I felt really paranoid."

TOBACCO

Other names for tobacco
Cigs, ciggies, fags, smoke.

What is it?
Tobacco comes from the tobacco plant. It contains a highly addictive drug called nicotine.

What does it look like?
Tobacco looks like brown leaves that have been dried and shredded into very small pieces.

How is it used?
Tobacco is smoked in a cigarette, roll-up (a cigarette that people make themselves) or pipe. Sometimes, people chew tobacco.

The law
It is illegal in Great Britain to sell tobacco products to anyone under the age of 18. Even so, by the age of 11, one in three children has experimented with smoking.

Why do people smoke?
People smoke for all sorts of reasons. Even though tobacco is a stimulant, many people feel that smoking helps them to relax and cope with stress. Some people smoke because they feel bored or lonely. Others use smoking to meet and talk to new people; cigarettes can help them to feel more confident. Some people smoke because they think it will help them to stay thin. Others simply enjoy smoking when they want to have a moment to themselves.

An early start

People usually start smoking when they are young. They often feel curious, and want to experiment and to try something new. They may smoke because their friends or people in their family smoke. They may believe that there is nothing wrong with smoking, and want to be like them, too. If a friend dares them to smoke, they may do it just so they do not look scared or because they want to fit in. They may want to show off in front of their friends, or they may just want to be the same as the people they hang out with.

In Great Britain, about 450 children start smoking every day. Many of these are girls.

'My dad smokes and I wish he didn't. What can I say to make him want to give up cigarettes?'

You could tell him that cigarettes contain more than 4000 different chemicals, including carbon monoxide, tar, acetone and cadmium. Carbon monoxide is a poisonous gas. It does not smell, and it is found in car exhaust pipes. Tar is a brown, sticky substance containing many poisonous chemicals. It sticks on tiny hairs inside the lungs that are designed to keep the lungs clean. This makes their job much harder! Acetone is used in nail varnish remover, and cadmium is used in batteries.

Research has found that more than 40 of the poisonous chemicals found in cigarettes cause cancer. When people puff on a cigarette, they draw all these chemicals into their lungs and around their body.

There is lots of help available to people who want to stop smoking. When your dad decides he is ready to give up cigarettes, your encouragement will really help him.

Excitement and rebellion

Young people may think that smoking makes them look cool, especially if the famous people they admire are smokers. Smoking can make young people feel independent and grown-up. Because some people say that smoking is wrong, they may want to rebel, and to do the opposite of what they are told.

Advertising can make smoking seem exciting. Tobacco companies often specifically target young people. Back in 1973, one tobacco company said, 'If our company is to survive and prosper, we must get our share of the youth market.' These companies know that, if young people smoke when they are young, they will probably continue to smoke as adults.

The risks of smoking

People who smoke may feel sick or dizzy. Nicotine in tobacco makes people's hearts beat faster and makes their arteries smaller. Smokers may find exercise difficult, because the chemicals in cigarettes reduce the amount of oxygen in their body. This makes them get breathless very quickly.

It's a Fact

- In the UK in 1994, children aged 11-15 smoked over one thousand million cigarettes, which cost them more than £135 million to buy.

So-called 'passive smoking', when people inhale the smoke from other people's cigarettes, can cause serious health problems.

People who smoke regularly often have bad breath, and their fingers turn yellowish-brown. Because nicotine makes people's skin age, they start to look old early on. A pregnant woman who smokes may lose her baby, or the baby may be born very small and with health problems.

Smoking causes lung diseases, such as asthma and chest infections. It also leads to heart disease and several kinds of cancer. About half of all people who smoke will die from smoking-related illnesses.

Nicotine is so addictive that, once people start smoking, it can be difficult for them to stop. Smoking is an expensive habit: over a lifetime, a smoker can spend many thousands of pounds on cigarettes.

Help yourself

Even though tobacco is all around us, it is one of the most addictive drugs there is. Don't get hooked – don't light up!

This picture shows a healthy lung (on the left) next to a diseased lung that has been damaged by smoking.

What Would you do?

Your friends keep trying to get you to smoke with them. Do you:

a) Say thanks, but you don't want to start smoking because it's unhealthy and expensive.

b) Get angry and shout at them that they're stupid.

c) Try one cigarette and then say you don't like it.

Turn to page 47 for the answers.

DEPRESSANTS

Depressants, or 'downers', slow people down, and make them feel drowsy and relaxed. This section of the book looks at some of the most common depressants: alcohol, cannabis and volatile substances.

It's a Fact

Other names for alcohol
Booze, bevvies.

What is it?
Alcohol is a liquid that contains a chemical called ethanol. Ethanol makes people feel tipsy or drunk when they consume alcoholic drinks.

What does it look like?
Alcohol is found in hundreds of drinks, such as beer, wine, alcopops and spirits (for example, vodka, whisky and rum).

How is it used?
Most alcohol is taken as a drink. Some people make jelly with vodka instead of water, and eat it.

ALCOHOL

The law
It is legal for adults to drink alcohol, but young people under 18 cannot buy alcohol. In the UK, 16- and 17-year-olds can drink beer, cider or wine with a meal in a bar or restaurant as long as it is bought for them by an adult who is with them.

Why do people drink alcohol?

People often use alcohol to unwind, relax and have fun. Alcohol can make people lose their inhibitions. They feel more friendly and chatty, confident and relaxed. Some people enjoy feeling tipsy or drunk and like the feeling of losing control.

Young people often use alcohol because it is quite cheap and easy to get hold of. They may drink because their friends are doing it, and they don't want to 'miss out' or look stupid.

WHAT'S THE PROBLEM?

'My sister is 16. When she goes out with her friends, they all drink alcohol. I'm worried about the amount they drink. How much is too much?'

The amount of alcohol in a drink is measured in units. Each unit contains 10ml of ethanol. One unit of alcohol equals:

- half a pint of beer, lager or cider
- one small glass of wine
- a single measure of spirits.

The UK government advises that the safe limits of alcohol for adults are:

- no more than 3-4 units a day for men
- no more than 2-3 units a day for women.

In addition, everyone should have one or two alcohol-free days a week.

There are **no** safe limits for young people under 18. Young people's bodies are still developing, and alcohol can damage this development.

When people are drunk they can lose control very quickly and may need help from others even to stand or walk. This can make young people vulnerable to predatory adults.

They may like the taste of some drinks, especially alcopops, which are designed to taste like soft drinks.

Some people use alcohol to cope with anxiety or stress, or because they feel lonely, depressed or bored. They think that alcohol will help them to escape from their problems. However, because alcohol is a depressant, it can actually make people feel worse.

Dangerous drinking

In some countries, binge drinking is a big problem. This is when people – young people, especially – drink just so they can get really drunk. They may mix different types of alcoholic drinks, or mix alcohol with other drugs. This is very dangerous, and can be life-threatening.

The risks of drinking alcohol

Because alcohol is a depressant, it slows down people's heart rate and their breathing. They may find it to hard to find words, and they slur their speech. They may become clumsy, stumbling or falling over when they try to walk. Even though they may feel very tired, they may not be able to sleep.

If someone drinks too much, they may collapse. As their body tries to get rid of the poisonous ethanol, they may be physically sick, and they can choke on their own vomit. Alcohol poisoning, when the body cannot cope with the amount of alcohol someone has drunk, can kill.

Alcohol can ruin relationships. When people are drunk, they are more likely to argue and to say things that they are sorry for later. They may become aggressive and violent.

Fights can start up when young people have been drinking alcohol.

People who are drunk often take more risks and put themselves in danger. In fact, anyone who is drunk is more likely to be robbed or to have an accident. It only takes a small amount of alcohol to affect coordination, and drinking and driving – even drinking and riding a bike – is very

Help yourself

Make sure you know how to help if someone you are with is very drunk:

- Give them a non-alcoholic drink, such as water or fruit juice.
- Never leave them alone.
- Get help as quickly as you can.

dangerous. Some people commit crimes when they are drunk.

Longer-term effects

Drinking too much alcohol can increase the risk of certain types of cancer, such as stomach, mouth and breast cancer. Because alcohol increases people's blood pressure, it can lead to a stroke or heart attack. Alcohol can also cause liver damage and, because alcohol can damage the lining of the stomach, it can give people ulcers. Drinking too much can also cause brain damage.

People who drink regularly can become addicted to alcohol. These people are known as alcoholics. Being an alcoholic ruins people's lives and has a devastating effect on the lives of those around them.

It's a Fact

- In the UK, about 150,000 people are taken into hospital every year because of alcohol-related accidents and illnesses.

HAVE YOUR SAY

"When I was 15 I went out and drank loads of vodka with my friends. I got so drunk I couldn't walk, then I passed out. My friends called an ambulance and I was rushed to hospital. When I woke up the nurse told me I could have died from alcohol poisoning. It was really scary. I never want to do that again."

CANNABIS

Other names for cannabis

Blow, dope, draw, ganja, hash, herbal, joint, marijuana, puff, skunk, spliff, wacky backy, weed.

What is it?

Cannabis is the most widely used illegal drug in the UK. It is a product of a bushy plant called hemp, which grows all over the world. Hemp has been used for hundreds of years to make items such as clothes, mats, rope, cooking oil and make-up.

Cannabis contains a chemical called THC, which is what gives cannabis users a 'high'.

Skunk is a very strong form of cannabis. It has a powerful smell. More and more young people nowadays are using skunk.

The effects – and the risks – of using skunk are even higher than other forms of cannabis.

What does it look like?

Cannabis comes in two main forms: resin and grass. Resin usually looks like small, brown lumps. Grass is the dried, shredded flowers, leaves, stalks and seeds of the cannabis plant. It looks like greenish-brown or grey tobacco. Skunk is a form of cannabis grass that can be 2-3 times stronger than other forms of cannabis.

The law

Cannabis is currently a Class C drug, but it will become a Class B drug from early 2009 if the reclassification is approved by Parliament.

How do people use cannabis?

Cannabis is often combined with tobacco and made into a 'joint' or 'spliff', which looks similar to a cigarette. It can also be smoked on its own in a special pipe, called a 'bong'. Some people mix cannabis with food and eat it; they may bake cannabis cakes or cookies, for example. Cannabis can also be made into a drink like tea.

How does cannabis make people feel?

Cannabis often makes people feel more relaxed, happy and friendly. People may have more energy, and talk and giggle a lot when they have used cannabis. Colours, taste, music and other sounds can seem sharper, brighter and better.

If people use a lot of cannabis at one time, they may have mild hallucinations. If they mix cannabis with other drugs, such as alcohol, they may feel sick and vomit. These effects can last for 2-8 hours.

Why do young people use cannabis

Young people may try cannabis because they are curious about what it is like. They may have friends who use cannabis, and want to join in with them. They may do it out of boredom or because they do not have anything better to do. They may enjoy the risk of doing something they know their parents would not approve of.

- In the UK, one in every five 16- to 24-year-olds uses cannabis.

People may think that cannabis is a relatively safe drug, because it is 'natural' – but cannabis use can cause serious physical and psychological consequences.

The risks of using cannabis

Some people believe that it is better to use cannabis than other drugs, such as alcohol or Ecstasy, because the hangover or comedown is not as bad. They may think that cannabis does not make people aggressive, which alcohol sometimes does. However, some people who use cannabis have mood swings. They may become worried or anxious, or even paranoid – thinking that people are talking about them or want to hurt them. Cannabis can make some people aggressive.

HAVE YOUR SAY

"I used cannabis for the first time with a mate, and I suddenly got really angry with him and said some awful stuff. I feel terrible about it."

Short-term effects

Cannabis can make a person's mouth and throat feel dry, and give them bloodshot eyes. Cannabis users often get the 'munchies', which means that they crave certain foods or drinks. They may also feel sick and dizzy.

They may vomit, especially if they have also used alcohol.

Sometimes, people who have used cannabis may get confused. It can be hard for them to remember things that have just happened. They are more likely to have accidents, even when doing simple things such as crossing the road. If cannabis makes them aggressive, they may do or say things they regret later on.

When people use cannabis, they may raid the kitchen for food to satisfy the 'munchies'.

Long-term effects

Some people believe that cannabis is not dangerous, because it comes from a natural plant. But cannabis contains chemicals just like other drugs, and these can harm the body and mind. These effects can be worse for young people whose brains are not yet fully developed.

Cannabis increases the heart rate and blood pressure, leading to heart problems. If people make cannabis joints with tobacco, their risk of getting smoking-related illnesses, such as asthma, chest infections, heart disease and cancer, gets higher. They may also become addicted to the nicotine in tobacco.

Studies have shown that people who use cannabis may find it harder to have a baby when they decide to start a family. If a woman uses cannabis when she is pregnant, the baby can be harmed.

Social and mental health problems

People who use cannabis can find it hard to concentrate or be motivated. The drug makes it harder for them to learn and remember things. Young people may fall behind at school. They may feel tired and have no energy, so they stop doing activities they used to enjoy. Cannabis can also cause mental health problems, such as depression, or make them worse.

Some people become addicted to cannabis. They may start to use stronger types of cannabis to get the same high. Some cannabis users go on to use other drugs, such as cocaine or heroin.

Cannabis can make some people become anxious or paranoid, and they may need professional help to overcome these problems.

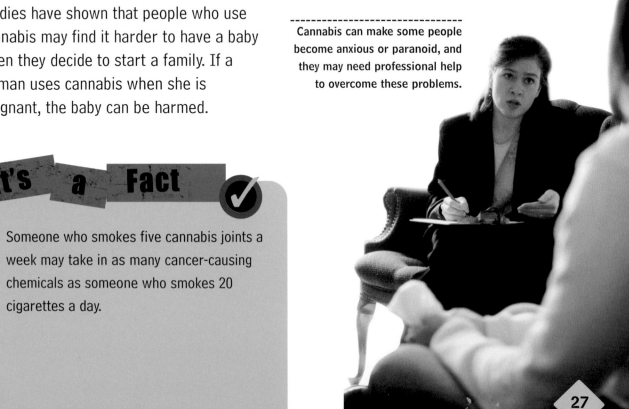

It's a Fact ✓

- Someone who smokes five cannabis joints a week may take in as many cancer-causing chemicals as someone who smokes 20 cigarettes a day.

VOLATILE SUBSTANCES

What are volatile substances?

They are ordinary household products, such as gas lighter refills; aerosols containing products such as hairspray, deodorant and air fresheners; nail varnish; tins or tubes of glue; some paints, thinners and correcting fluids.

What do they look like?

Examples of volatile substances that people use to get high include model aeroplane glue, nail polish remover, cleaning fluids, hairspray and spray paint.

How are they used?

Volatile substances are sniffed or breathed into the lungs from a cloth, sleeve or plastic bag. Gas products are sometimes squirted into the back of the throat.

What do they feel like?

People who use volatile substances can feel very excited and happy. They may have slurred speech and loss of concentration, as if they are very drunk. Some people have hallucinations while using volatile substances.

The effects of volatile substances do not last a long time. However, people can keep the effects going all day by using more and more of the drug.

What are the short-term risks?

Volatile substances can make people feel sick and vomit. They may feel light-headed and have hallucinations. They may suffocate,

Every household has chemicals in the form of common products, such as hairspray, glue and paint. Misusing these chemicals can be very dangerous indeed.

especially if they inhale volatile substances using a plastic bag. They may become unconscious, and some people have a heart attack and die immediately.

People who are high on volatile substances are at greater risk of having an accident. Using volatile substances with alcohol or other drugs makes this even more likely.

After using volatile substances, people may feel sleepy for a few hours. They may have a headache. People who repeat doses of volatile substances to stay high are at greater risk of losing consciousness and death.

What are the long-term risks?

People who use volatile substances for a long time may lose weight and have weak muscles. They may find it hard to concentrate or pay attention. They may be irritable or depressed. Over time, volatile substances can damage people's brain, liver and kidneys. Risk of addiction to volatile substances is high.

The law

It is illegal for people under 18 to buy gas lighter refills, gases, glues and aerosols. Even so, sniffing volatile drugs is more common among 11-12-year-olds than older children and adults.

What Would you do?

You've been sniffing volatile substances, and your mum finds some lighter gas in your room. Your parents get really angry. Do you:

a) Lie to them by pretending that you don't know anything about it.
b) Wait until your parents calm down, and then explain why you started using drugs.
c) Go to a friend's house and refuse to go home.

Turn to page 47 for the answers.

HALLUCINOGENS AND ANALGESICS

Hallucinogens, or 'trips', make people hallucinate, which means that they see or hear things that are not really there. Analgesics have a pain-killing effect. These pages explore the most common hallucinogen, LSD, and analgesic, heroin.

LSD

Other names for LSD
Acid, blotters, dots, microdots, tabs, trips.

What is it?
LSD is a synthetic drug, made from a type of fungus.

What does it look like?
LSD comes as very small paper squares, often with a picture on them. Microdots and dots are tiny tablets. LSD can also come as a clear liquid or on small squares of gelatin.

How is it used?
LSD is often sucked and then swallowed. It can also be injected. Gelatin and liquid can be put into the eyes.

What does it feel like?
LSD causes hallucinations, or 'trips', which can last for 8-12 hours. People may see unusual shapes and extra-bright colours. Sometimes, they hear strange noises. Objects may look as if they are changing. Movement and time may seem to speed up or slow down.

What are the short-term risks?
When someone has used LSD, their heart beats faster and their blood pressure goes up. Users can feel hot, sick or dizzy. They may have a dry mouth and lose their appetite. They can have mood swings and feel panicky. Once a trip has started, it cannot be stopped. A bad trip can be long and terrifying.

What are the long-term risks?
LSD users can have flashbacks, when they suddenly see or hear things from previous LSD trips. This can happen within a few days of taking LSD, or up to a year afterwards. People who use LSD a lot can become mentally ill.

The law
LSD is a Class A drug.

HEROIN

Other names for heroin

Brown, gear, H, horse, jack, junk, smack, skag.

What is it?

Heroin is an analgesic drug, which comes from the opium poppy.

What does it look like?

Heroin usually comes as an off-white, brownish powder, usually wrapped in small packets of paper.

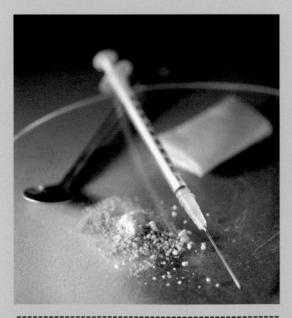

Heroin is an extremely addictive drug. Once in its grip, it can be hard for people to break a heroin habit.

How is it used?

Heroin is dissolved and injected into a vein or muscle. It can also be smoked, inhaled as smoke through a straw or sniffed as powder through the nose.

What does it feel like?

Heroin can make people feel warm and give them a great sense of well-being. Some people feel drowsy, relaxed and 'apart' from the real world. People's speech may slow down and be slurred. They may move slowly and their eyelids may be droopy.

What are the short-term risks?

People who use heroin for the first time can feel sick and dizzy. Heroin stops people from being able to cough, and people can die from inhaling their own vomit. Some people overdose on heroin, and can go into a coma or die.

What are the long-term risks?

Long-term heroin users may develop lung, liver, kidney or brain problems. Heroin is highly addictive. People may need to carry on using this drug just to feel normal.

The law

Heroin is a Class A drug.

PROBLEM DRUG USE

'I'm addicted to chocolate!' 'I'm addicted to this TV programme!' People often talk about their 'addictions'. Most of the time, these things are not harmful. Drug addiction, however, is a much more serious matter.

People use drugs for all sorts of reasons. They may start by experimenting with drugs. They may go on to use drugs for fun, which is called recreational drug use. When people first try drugs, the last thing on their mind is addiction. Addiction is something that happens to 'other people'. But all drugs – legal or illegal – can be addictive.

What is problem drug use?

Problem drug use is when people need to use a drug just to cope with day-to-day life. Problem drug users use more drugs, more often, than other drug users. Drugs might have been 'fun' for a while – but they turn into something much darker. Problem drug users think about drugs all the time. The trouble is that no one knows whether this might happen to them until it is too late.

It can be hard – and even painful – to stop using drugs. But, whereas the pain of withdrawal lasts only a short time, the benefits of quitting last a lifetime.

'My mates told me that it's OK to use cannabis because it's not addictive like heroin. Are they right?'

Some drugs, such as heroin, are physically addictive. Others, such as cannabis, are not physically addictive, but are psychologically addictive. Some people may choose to use drugs that are not physically addictive, because they think this is better. But psychological addiction is just as serious and as hard to beat as physical addiction.

What is drug addiction?

Drugs contain chemicals that change the way someone's body or mind works. Over time, some drugs can change a person's brain, so that it stops making its own natural 'feel-good' chemicals.

At this point, people need to keep using the drugs to make themselves feel better – or even normal. This is physical addiction. When people stop using drugs they are physically addicted to, they can experience nasty withdrawal symptoms, such as pain or vomiting.

Physical and psychological

Some drugs do not cause physical addiction – but most drugs can cause psychological addiction. This means that someone is dependent on using a drug to make them feel good. If they stop using the drug, they may feel that they cannot cope. These feelings can be very strong.

People who are addicted to drugs use them even though they know that they are damaging their health and ruining their lives. They cannot control their drug use. Instead, the drugs control them.

HAVE YOUR SAY

"I'm hooked on cigarettes. I can stop smoking for a short while but there's always something that stresses me out and I start up again. I can't stop. And I know it could kill me."

Why do some people become addicted to drugs?

Not everyone who uses drugs will become a drug addict. However, there are some things that might make this more likely.

Family background

We all have genes that we inherit from our parents. If someone in our family has a problem with addiction, it is more likely that we will, too. Someone with an alcoholic parent is four times more likely to become an alcoholic themselves.

Children who have been abused or neglected sometimes turn to drugs to escape from their problems and fears, and are more likely to become addicted, too.

Mental illness and stress

People who have a mental health problem, such as depression or anxiety, may become addicted to drugs. If someone cannot cope with stress, this can also make them vulnerable. Using drugs may be the only way they feel they can cope.

Part of everyday life

In some places, drug use is seen as normal. Perhaps someone at home drinks a lot or uses cannabis. Drugs are sometimes linked to fashion, music and dance — and so some young people use drugs frequently. This puts people at greater risk of addiction.

- Ninety-five per cent of people who are addicted to drugs started to use them before they were 20 years old. The younger someone is when they first use drugs, the more likely they are to become an addict.

Sometimes, people use drugs to escape from problems such as bullying.

WORRIED ABOUT SOMEONE?

Worrying that someone we care about is using drugs is hard. Will they try to make us use drugs, too? What will happen to them? Will they die? Questions like these can race around our minds.

Warning signs

Different drugs produce different effects on people. However, there are some things to watch out for that might suggest that someone is using drugs.

Some people who use drugs have a runny nose or bloodshot eyes. They may stop eating or sleeping, or eat or sleep a lot. They may not care about what they look like. Drug users can become moody. They may seem angry, depressed or jittery. It might be hard for them to concentrate.

People who use drugs sometimes fall out with their old friends, and start hanging out with new people. They may tell lies or hide things. They may avoid their family, and stop doing activities they used to enjoy.

Some drug users ask for money a lot. They may keep 'losing' their belongings, or start stealing. Unusual equipment – such as burnt foil and cigarette packets – in a person's room, bag or clothes can also be a sign that someone is using drugs.

Problem drug users can look pale and ill.

HAVE YOUR SAY

"When my brother went out one day, mum decided to clean his room. That's when she found a dark brown lump wrapped in cling film under his pillow. It turned out to be cannabis resin."

Living with an addict

It can be especially difficult if a family member, such as a parent, abuses drugs. These parents may not look after their children properly. They may lose their job or have money troubles. They may argue a lot, and it can be hard for children to bring friends home.

Some children feel guilty if their parent has a drug problem. But a parent's drug use is **never** the child's fault. Children may feel lonely, worried and scared. It is important to remember that we are never alone. Children cannot make a parent stop using drugs – but there are lots of ways to get help and support. (See page 37 for more information.)

Children who have a drug-using parent should try to take care of themselves. Doing fun, healthy activities can help them to feel better and stronger. Knowing how to stay safe – by phoning the emergency services, for example – is important. It is also important to talk to someone we trust – ideally, to an adult. This person may be able to help the drug user to get the professional help they need.

It is very distressing to watch someone we love ruin their lives with drugs.

It's a Fact

- Between 200,000 and 300,000 children in England and Wales have one or both parents with serious drug problems.

GETTING HELP

It can be very hard for people to admit that they have a problem with drugs. Young people, especially, often believe that it will never happen to them. They may think that problem drug users are drop-outs who live on the streets. However, anyone who uses drugs risks drug problems.

Some people pretend that they do not use drugs, or say that they do not use drugs a lot. Hiding the truth can make them cut themselves off from friends and family. This leaves them feel lonely and afraid – and makes everything worse.

Often, people think they have to be a drug addict to have a drug problem. This is far from the truth. If anyone feels their life is changing or getting worse because of their drug use, they may have a problem with drugs. Perhaps they are falling behind at school, or losing touch with the people who really care about them.

Anyone who is even slightly worried about their drug use can get help. No one has to suffer alone.

HAVE YOUR SAY

"At first, using a bit of coke was just a laugh. Then I wasn't getting the same kind of high, so I tried crack. Before I knew it, all I could think of was getting my next fix."

"Smoking dope is something I do with my mates. My family don't know I do it, and I don't want them to know."

First steps

The first step towards getting help is accepting that there is a problem in the first place. If someone does not accept that they have a problem with drugs, there is no way that they can find the support they need.

WHAT'S THE PROBLEM?

'How do I know if I have a problem with drugs?'

First of all, you need to be honest with yourself. Think about the questions below carefully. Write down your answers, if you like.

- Do you think about drugs a lot?
- Do you only go to places where people might have drugs?
- Have you lost touch with your old friends?
- Are you struggling to keep up at school because you're tired or you can't concentrate?

- Are you bored with things you used to do? Does taking drugs seem much more exciting?
- Have you stopped caring about what you look like?

If one or more of your answers is 'Yes', your drug use might be becoming a problem. Don't worry – you are not alone. You can find the help you need.

As soon as a drug user is ready, help is available. It may not always be easy to stop using drugs – but many thousands of people quit successfully, and lead full and happy lives.

Who can help?

Some drug users are able to overcome their drug problem on their own. However, most drug users need support from other people in order to stop using drugs. This help can come from many places, such as family, friends, doctors and professional organizations.

It is pretty safe to say that our families love us. If someone feels they have a drug problem, talking to parents is usually a great starting point. It helps to stay calm and to explain quietly exactly what the problem is. Parents may seem worried or shocked, but they will pleased and relieved to have been asked for help. They may not be able to deal with the problem themselves, but they will be able to help their child to find the professional help they need.

If someone finds it too difficult to open up to their parents, they could talk to a trusted friend or adult, such as a teacher, school nurse, youth worker or doctor. Doctors can provide regular check-ups and support for drug users.

Parents can give loving support to their children, and can help them to talk to professionals to help them to overcome their drug problem.

HAVE YOUR SAY

"I thought my mum and dad would go ballistic, but they listened to me really carefully. They said they'd go to see the doctor with me. It was such a relief to talk to them."

Sometimes, it can be easier to speak to someone we do not know if we have a problem. Some towns and cities have drop-in centres, which give advice and help for drug users. There are some excellent national organizations, too. They offer confidential advice and support. Turn to page 47 for more information.

There are many reasons why people use drugs or develop drug problems. Some people have personal, relationship or emotional problems. They may be suffering neglect or abuse at home or school.

Some schools have trained counsellors to talk to about these issues. It can help people to make the deep changes required in order to stop using drugs.

Some people with drug problems go to rehabilitation centres which offer practical help and support to overcome addiction. People can attend daily or stay in a rehabilitation centre for several weeks.

Help yourself

Finding help

If you think you or one of your friends has a problem with drugs, don't wait. Get help now! Page 47 has a list of useful helplines and websites, which are a good place to start seeking help and support.

Remember – everyone can overcome drug problems. There are lots of places to go for help. Life can get better and better.

Breaking a drug habit can open the way for fun, healthy living, such as trying out a team sport like basketball to play with others.

IN AN EMERGENCY

Drug use is becoming more common among young people. Drugs can affect people in different ways, and can make people very ill. Some drugs, such as volatile substances and heroin, make people drowsy. They may even become unconscious. Other drugs, such as cannabis, Ecstasy and LSD, can make people anxious or panicky. Drugs such as Ecstasy can make people too hot and dehydrated.

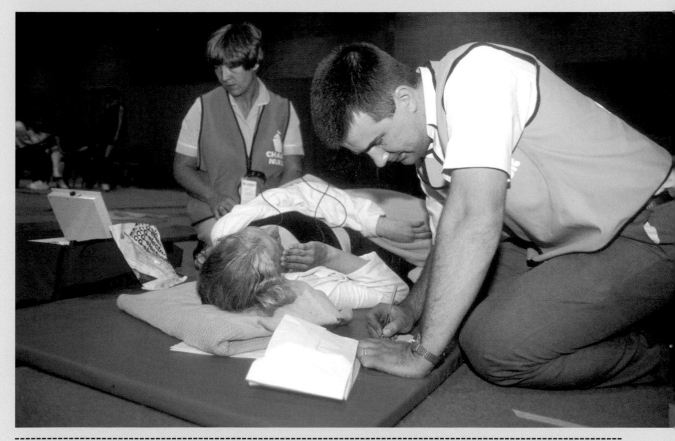

Never hesitate to call the emergency services for help if someone is badly affected by drugs.

It is important to know what to do in different situations. Emergencies are rare, but it is a good idea to know how to handle them. First of all, it is important not to panic. Try to find out what drugs the person has used. If you are very worried about them, call for help. If you have a mobile phone, dial 999 and ask for an ambulance. Do not leave the person alone and stay with them until help arrives.

Help yourself

Know what to do and what not to do in an emergency

If someone is drowsy
If possible, take them to a place where there is cool, fresh air.

Try to keep them still and quiet, but awake.

Speak to them quietly and calmly, so they do not get frightened.

Never throw water over them or give them coffee to wake them up.

If they stay drowsy, if you know how to do this, place them on their side in the recovery position. It's a very good idea to find out how to do this — it could help you to save someone's life. The website of the British Red Cross has a detailed explanation of how to put someone in the recovery position. See page 47 for the website address.

If someone is unconscious
Dial 999 immediately, and ask for an ambulance.

If you know how to do this, place them on their side in the recovery position.

Stay with them until the ambulance crew arrives.

Tell the ambulance crew what drugs have been taken, if you know this.

If someone is getting panicky
Take them somewhere quiet.

Keep them away from lots of people, bright lights and loud noises.

Try to calm them down. Tell them quietly that they will soon feel better.

If they are breathing very quickly, tell them to take long, slow breaths.

If someone is too hot and dehydrated
If possible, take them to a place where there is cool, fresh air.

Take off any clothes that may be making them hotter.

Give them non-alcoholic drinks, such as water or fruit juice, to sip slowly — but no more than one pint an hour.

MAKING THE RIGHT CHOICES

Everyone has the choice whether to use drugs or not. No one can make anyone else become a drug user, even though they might try to. Learning about drugs, their effects and the problems they can bring is a great way to make sensible, informed choices.

It is important not to rely on friends for facts about drugs – they may not know as much as you, or they, think they know. There are some excellent websites and books which have accurate and up-to-date information about drugs (see page 47). Reading this book is a great start!

Everyone reacts differently to different drugs. It all depends on what the person is like, where they are – and even the mood they are in when they use drugs. One person might be able to walk away from drugs quite easily. Someone else might end up ruining their life as a drug addict. Before taking the risk, isn't it better to know what the deal is?

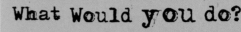

What Would you do?

Your friends are into drugs. You're tempted to try them but, first, you want to find out more. Do you:

a) Ask your friends what they think about drugs.
b) Go to the library or Internet to read up about drugs.
c) Decide it's too much hassle, so just try the drugs, anyway.

Turn to page 47 for the answers.

Being knowledgeable about drugs can help people to make the right choices – and avoid the horrible consequences of making the wrong choices.

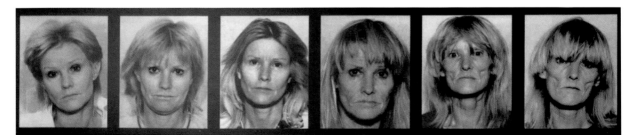

DON'T LET DRUG DEALERS CHANGE THE FACE OF YOUR NEIGHBOURHOOD.
Call Crimestoppers anonymously on 0800 555 111.

Pressure, pressure, pressure!

It is normal to want to fit in with friends and to do what they do. But this can lead to bad choices. Would you run towards the edge of a cliff, just because your friends are doing it? Using drugs can be just as dangerous. It is important to make our own choices about our lives, for our own reasons.

Saying 'No' to drugs can be hard, especially if there is a lot of peer pressure. However, there are ways to make this easier.

First, choose friends carefully. A good friend is someone who enjoys the same things as us, shares our values and respects our decisions. Friends who pressurize others to use drugs are not true friends at all. Be informed! Getting accurate information about drugs helps people to be clear about

what they think and to stick to their views. Remember — most people respect others who refuse to 'go with the flow'. And, if something does not **feel** right, then it is **not** right.

Help yourself

Saying 'No'

Be calm, clear and confident when you say 'No' to drugs. This will help to stop people getting pushy.

If someone is worried about peer pressure, it can help to talk about it with a trusted friend or adult. There is always someone to help.

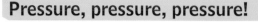

Choosing friends who share the same interests can help to prevent people 'getting into the wrong crowd'.

Know the facts

Some people think that whether or not to use drugs is a clear-cut issue. They say that drugs are bad and using drugs is wrong. But the issue is more complicated than that. Drugs can be dangerous and they can ruin people's lives. But some people enjoy using drugs and they stay in control.

So, to recap:

- Some people use drugs because they are curious.
- Some people use drugs because they want to have fun.
- Some people use drugs because they want to escape from problems.
- Drugs can give people a good feeling for a while.
- The effects of drugs can be really horrible.
- Some people use drugs carefully, and quitting is not hard for them.

- Some people end up as drug addicts.
- No one can know from the start whether they will become a problem drug user or not.
- Most drugs are illegal. Even legal drugs are illegal for young people.
- Drugs can make people very ill.
- Drugs can ruin people's lives.
- Drugs can kill.

Whether or not someone uses drugs is a personal decision. However, making that decision without honest, accurate information is foolish.

It's a Fact

- In recent years in the UK, levels of drug use among 11-15-year-olds has gone down.

Glossary

abuse when someone hurts another person emotionally, physically or sexually

addiction when someone cannot stop using drugs

AIDS acquired immune deficiency syndrome, the final stage of HIV infection

alcoholic someone who is addicted to alcohol

analgesic a drug that has a pain-killing effect on the body

anxiety feelings of worry and nervousness about something that might happen

binge drinking when someone drinks several alcoholic drinks within a short period of time

coma a deep state of unconsciousness, often caused by brain damage

comedown the effects people experience when a drug has left their body

confidential secret

counsellor someone who is trained to listen to people and give them advice about their problems

dehydrated when too much water has been lost from someone's body

depressant a drug that slows down people's bodies, making them feel drowsy and relaxed. Depressant drugs are sometimes called 'downers'

drug dealer someone who gives or sells drugs to someone else

fine an amount of money to be paid because someone has done something illegal

hallucinate when someone sees or hear things that are not really there. The experience, or hallucination, is sometimes called a 'trip'

hallucinogen a drug that makes people hallucinate

hangover the symptoms people feel the day after drinking alcohol

hepatitis a serious disease of the liver

high blood pressure when blood is flowing too quickly in someone's body

HIV human immunodeficiency virus, the virus that causes AIDS

inhale breathe in

mentally ill when someone has an illness of the mind, such as depression or anxiety

neglect when someone fails to look after the basic needs of a person for whom they are responsible

overdose to take more of a drug than the body can cope with

paranoid when someone has a strong, unreasonable feeling that people do not like them or want to hurt them

police conviction when the police find someone to be guilty of a crime

professional someone who is qualified and paid for the job they do

rehabilitation centre a place where drug users can go to recover from their addiction and become healthy

stimulant a drug that speeds up people's bodies, making them feel excited and on a 'high'. Stimulant drugs are sometimes called 'uppers'

suffocate be unable to breathe

ulcer a break in part of the body, which does not heal up

unconscious when a person has lost consciousness and is not awake

Further information

BOOKS

Jacqui Bailey, Talk About: Drugs, **Wayland, 2008**

Paul Mason, Know the Facts: Drinking and Smoking, **Wayland, 2008**

Jillian Powell, Emotional Health Issues: Alcohol and Drug Abuse, **Wayland, 2008**

Rachel Lynette, Drugs, **Heinemann Library, 2007**

Jane Bingham, What's the Deal?: Alcohol; Cannabis; Cocaine; Heroin; Smoking, **Heinemann Library, 2006**

Karla Fitzhugh, What's the Deal? Ecstasy; Steroids, **Heinemann Library, 2006**

USEFUL ORGANIZATIONS AND HELPLINES

Addaction – www.addaction.org.uk

Alateen – www.al-anon.alateen.org

ChildLine – www.childline.org.uk. Kidszone – www.childline.org.uk/Just4U.asp
Free telephone helpline: 0800 1111

D-World – www.drugscope-dworld.org.uk

FRANK – www.talktofrank.com.
Free telephone helpline: 0800 77 66 00.

Kids Against Tobacco Smoke – www.roycastle.org/kats

Lifebytes – www.lifebytes.gov.uk

Red Cross – Find out how to put someone in the recovery position. Go to: www.redcross.org.uk/standard.asp?id=56899

Sussed about Drink – www.sussedaboutdrink.net

WHAT WOULD YOU DO?

Page 9

a) Getting angry might make your friends get angry, too – and cause even more problems.

b) You may want to be liked and fit in, but buying alcohol when you are underage is illegal – not to mention dangerous!

c) You know right from wrong, and you are strong enough to state your feelings without attacking the other person.

Page 18

a) Staying calm and saying why you don't want to smoke can be a really good way to get friends off your back.

b) Insulting your friends might just make them more determined to get you to smoke. That way, they'll feel better about themselves.

c) You don't need to do something just because your friends do it. Stick to what you believe in!

Page 29

a) Your parents are likely to see through your lies. Do you really want them to stop trusting you?

b) This is the best plan. Being honest about your feelings will make it easier for you to get the help you need to stop using drugs. Your parents won't hate you!

c) Running away never solves anything. The problem won't go away.

Page 43

a) You know the answer before you get it! Your friends are bound to say that drugs are good, because they're taking them and want to look cool.

b) Good option! Get informed – then make your own decision based on the facts.

c) This could be risky. You don't know how the drugs might affect you, and you could be putting yourself in danger.

INDEX Numbers in bold refer to illustrations.

abuse 9, 34, 40

addiction 5, 10, 11, 19, 23, 27, 29, 31, 32, 33, 34, 36, 40, 43, 45

advertising 18

aerosols 6, 29, **29**

aggression 22, **22**, 26

AIDS 13

alcohol 4, 6, 7, 10, 20, **20**, 21, 22, 25, 26, 47

alcoholics 10, 23, 34

alcohol-related illnesses 10, 23

anabolic steroids 6, 12, 15

analgesics 7, 8, 30, 31, **31**

anxiety 10, 26, 34

binge drinking 21

caffeine 4, 6

cannabis 4, 6, 7, 8, 20, 24, 25, **25**, 26, 27, 33, 35, 41

cocaine 4, 6, 12, **12**, 27

counsellors 40

crack cocaine 12, 13, **13**

crime 4, 10, 23

dance 8, 14, 34

debt 10

depressants 7, 8, 20, **20**, 21, 22, **25**, **28**

doctors 6, 38, 39

'downers' 7, 20

drug dealers **5**, 6, 7

Ecstasy 4, 6, 8, 10, 12, 14, **14**, 26, 41

effects 5, 6, 7, 23, 26, 35, 43, 45, 47

emergency services 36, 41, **41**, 42

experimenting 8

fashion 8, 34

flashbacks 30

friends 4, 6, 9, 11, 17, 19, 21, 25, 36, 37, 38, 40, 43, 43, 44, **44**, 47

glues 6, **7**, **28**, 29

hallucinations 25, 28, 30

hallucinogens 7, 8, 30

hangovers 26

help 17, 36, 37, 38, 39, 40, 41, 42

hepatitis 13

heroin 4, 6, 7, 8, 27, 30, 31, **31**, 33, 41

HIV 13

illegal drugs 4, 5, 6, 11, 24, 45

law 7, 11, 12, 13, 14, 15, 16, 20, 24, 29, 30, 31

legal drugs 4, 5, 6, 45

LSD 6, 7, 8, 30, 41

magic mushrooms 7

medicines 4, 6

memory 11, 27

mental illness 10, 14, 27, 30, 34

methadone 7

mixing drugs 6, 21, 25, 29

music 8, 34

neglect 9, 34, 40

nicotine 16, 18, 19, 27

opium 5, 31

overdoses 10, 31

panic 10, 14

paranoia 10, 13, 15, 26

parents 25, 29, 34, 36, 39, 47

passive smoking **18**

police 7, 11

pressure 9, 18, 44

prison 7

rebellion 9, 18

rehabilitation centres 40

relationships 11, 22

risks 5, 10, 11, 12, 13, 14, 15, 19, 22, 23, 25, 26, 28, 29, 30, 31, 34, 47

saying 'No' 44, 45

school 6, 9, 11, 27, 37, 38, 40

self-esteem 9

signs of drug use 35, **35**

skunk 24

smoking-related illnesses 10, **10**, 19, **19**, 27

society 9

stimulants 6, 8, 12, **12**, **13**, 14, **14**, 16, **16**

stress 16, 21, 34

tobacco 4, 6, 9, 10, 12, 16, **16**, **17**, 18, **18**, 19, 24, 27, 47

'trips' 7, 8, 30

'uppers' 12

volatile substances 7, **7**, 10, 20, 28, **28**, 29, 33, 41

weight loss 9

withdrawal symptoms 33